Thomas Jefferson

by Darleen Ramos

Boston, Massachusetts
Chandler, Arizona
Glenview, Illinois
Upper Saddle River, New Jersey

Illustrations
3, 4 Bradley Clark.

Photographs
Every effort has been made to secure permission and provide appropriate credit for photographic material.
The publisher deeply regrets any omission and pledges to correct errors called to its attention in subsequent editions.

Unless otherwise acknowledged, all photographs are the property of Pearson Education, Inc.

Photo locators denoted as follows: Top (T), Center (C), Bottom (B), Left (L), Right (R), Background (Bkgd)

Opener: Getty Images; 1 Getty Images; 2 Medioimages/Photodisc/Thinkstock; 5 Photos to Go/Photolibrary; 6 Thinkstock; 7 Thinkstock; 8 Library of Congress; 9 Library of Congress; 10 Library of Congress; 11 National Archives; 12 Library of Congress; 13 Thinkstock; 14 Library of Congress; 15 Getty Images.

ISBN-13: 978-0-328-67605-7
ISBN-10:   0-328-67605-5

11 12 13 V0SI 18 17 16 15

This is Thomas Jefferson who helped start our country.

He was a writer, an inventor, as well as a president of the United States.

Jefferson was born in 1743.

His family was rich, and he grew up on a large farm in Virginia.

There were thirteen **colonies** then.

Great Britain ruled them and made the laws.

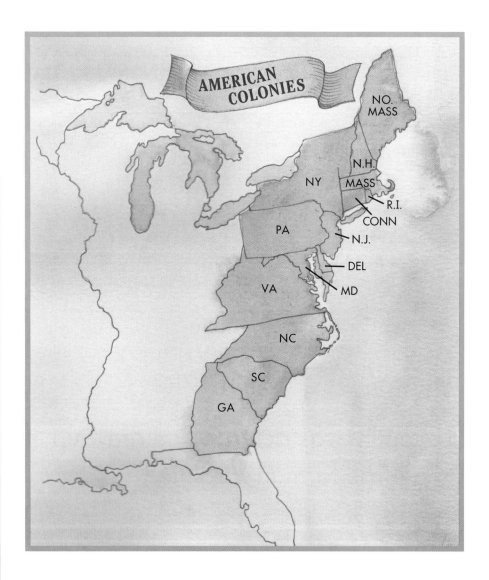

AMERICAN COLONIES

Jefferson studied hard as he grew up.

Later, Jefferson raised his family in a home he built.

He called it Monticello.

Jefferson was not a great speaker.

But he was a great writer.

He wrote that the colonies should be free from Great Britain.

Many colonists wanted their own **government**.

They began to protest in many ways.

They dumped tea into Boston Harbor.

In 1774, people from the colonies met in a **congress**.

Soon after, the Revolutionary War began.

A year later, Jefferson joined the second Congress.

He was asked to write a **declaration** that the colonies should be free.

It took weeks to write the Declaration of **Independence**.

Congress signed the declaration on July 4, 1776.

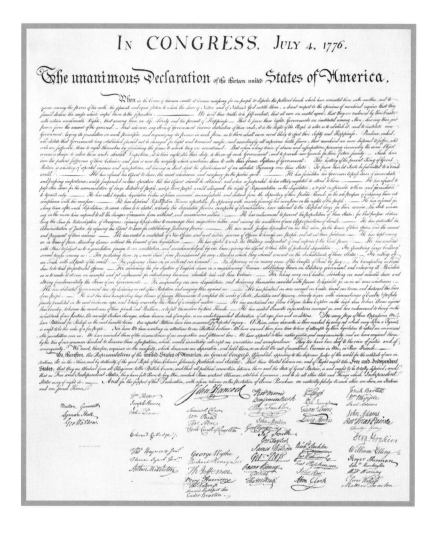

Jefferson's words in the declaration were powerful.

He wrote that "all men are created equal."

Finally, America won its war for independence.

George Washington asked Jefferson to be the first secretary of state.

In 1801, Jefferson was **elected** the third president of the United States.

President Jefferson had good ideas.

He purchased land from France.

The country was now twice as big.

Jefferson's words and ideas helped shape our country.

That was true then.

That is also true now.

Glossary

colonies settlements that are ruled by another country

congress a formal meeting to talk about issues

declaration a public statement

elected chosen by voters

government the leaders of a country or place

independence freedom